Read and Play
Kittens

by Jim Pipe

Stargazer Books
Mankato, Minnesota

kitten

A **kitten** is
a baby cat.

2

3

meow

A kitten
says **meow**.

4

5

fur

6

A kitten
has **fur**.

7

eye

8

A kitten has big **eyes**.

9

paw

10

A kitten has **paws**.

11

run

A kitten **runs**.

12

play

14

A kitten **plays**.

15

drink

16

A kitten **drinks**.

17

sleep

A kitten **sleeps**.
Good night!

19

What am I?

paw

mouth

eye

fur

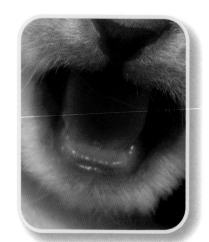

20

Match the words and pictures.

How many?

Can you count the kittens?

21

My Friends

Who is friends with these kittens?

Index

For Parents and Teachers

Questions you could ask:

p. 2 How many kittens can you see? These five kittens are drinking their mother's milk. You could also mention that when two or more kittens are born at the same time, it is known as a "litter."

p. 4 How big is a kitten? Note the hand holding the kitten in the picture for comparison. When it is born, a kitten weighs just 4 ounces (100 grams).

p. 6 What do you think a kitten's fur feels like? It is very soft and hairy. A cat cleans its kittens' fur by licking them. Kittens soon learn to lick themselves clean.

p. 8 Can you see the whiskers? The whiskers (long hairs) on a kitten's face help it to feel its way around.

p. 11 What is this kitten doing? It is climbing a tree—its sharp claws grip the trunk.

p. 12 What color are kittens? This kitten is orange —other kittens are black, brown, white, or gray.

p. 14 Do kittens like to play? Yes, they like to climb, jump, and sharpen their claws, and to hunt things like the toy mouse in this picture.

p. 16 What do kittens drink? Kittens do like milk but it is much better to give them a bowl of water.

Activities you could do:

• Introduce the topic with cat and kitten rhymes such as "Hey, Diddle, Diddle," "The Robber Kitten," and "Three Little Kittens" (which describes the behavior of kittens).

• Role play: ask the reader to show how they would care for a kitten (using a stuffed toy), e.g. feeding it and brushing it clean. Help them understand that a kitten is a living creature, not just a toy that can be put away.

• Help children to make kitten shapes from three pieces of modeling clay—one large ball for body, a smaller ball for head, and a longer, thinner piece for tail. Pinch clay to make ears and use toothpick to shape the eyes and create whisker holes.

• Play a game of "pin the tail" using a kitten picture.

© Aladdin Books Ltd 2009

Designed and produced by
Aladdin Books Ltd

First published in 2009 in the United States by
Stargazer Books,
distributed by
Black Rabbit Books
PO Box 3263
Mankato, MN 56002

Library of Congress Cataloging-in-Publication Data

Pipe, Jim, 1966-
  Kittens / Jim Pipe.
    p. cm. -- (Read and play)
    Summary: "In very simple language and photographs, describes kittens. Includes quizzes and games"--Provided by publisher.
    ISBN 978-1-59604-179-0
  1. Kittens--Juvenile literature. I. Title.
SF445.7.P565 2009
636.8'07--dc22

2008015300

Series consultant
Zoe Stillwell is an experienced preschool teacher.

Photocredits:
l-left, r-right, b-bottom, t-top, c-center, m-middle. All photos from istockphoto.com except: 4-5, 20tl, 23bl—Tony Campbell / Dreamstime.com. 8-9, 20tr, 23tml—Tina Rencelj / Dreamstime.com. 11 — Zoran Djekic / Dreamstime.com. 14-15, 23tmr—Amy Weiland / Dreamstime.com. 16-17, 23tl—Robyn Glover / Dreamstime.com.